LEVEL 2

Soccer

Melissa Santoyo

NATIONAL GEOGRAPHIC KiDS

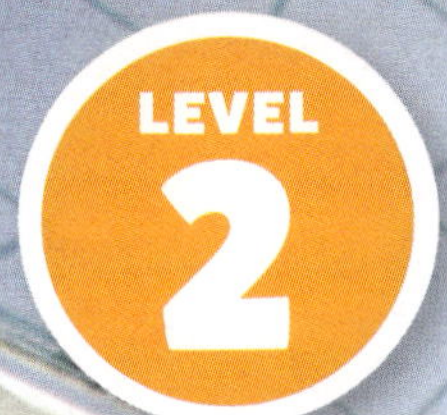

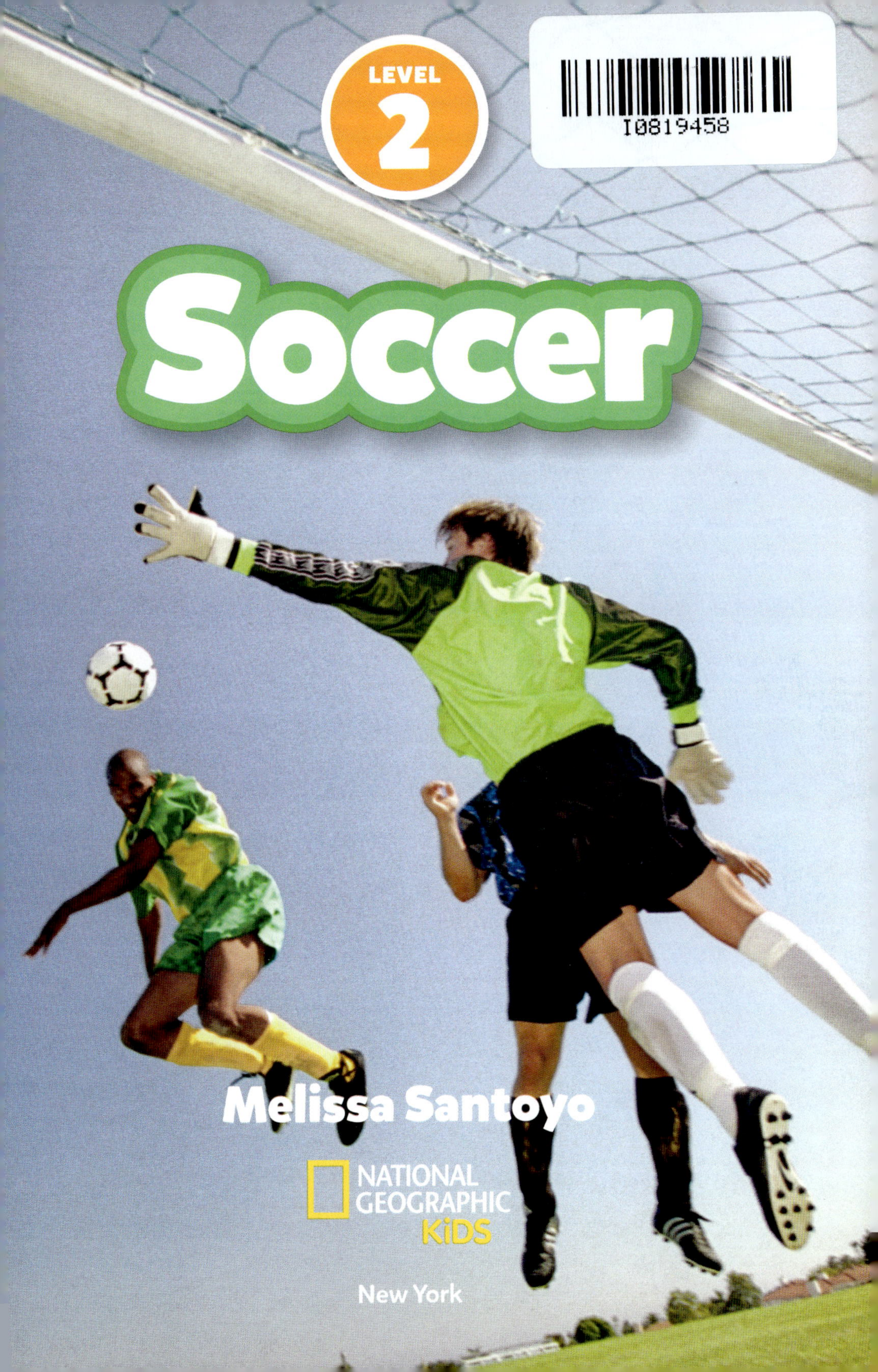

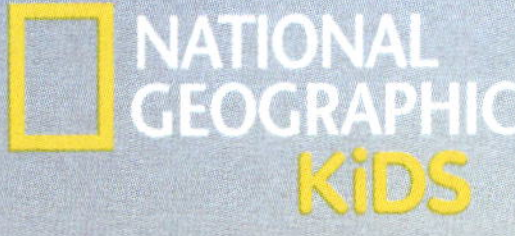

New York

For my brother Alvaro, who's always been the sportier one —M.S.

A National Geographic Kids Book
Published by Random House Children's Books under license.
A division of Penguin Random House LLC
1745 Broadway, New York, NY 10019
penguinrandomhouse.com
rhcbooks.com

Designed by Lauren Sciortino

The publisher would like to thank Dave Sanford, expert consultant and executive director and technical director at Gunston Soccer Club; Mariam Jean Dreher, literacy reviewer; and Michelle Harris, fact-checker.

Library of Congress Cataloging-in-Publication Data is available upon request.
ISBN 978-1-4263-7802-7 (trade paperback) –
ISBN 978-1-4262-2495-9 (lib. bdg)

Manufactured in the United States of America
10 9 8 7 6 5 4 3 2

The authorized representative in the EU for product safety and compliance is Penguin Random House Ireland, Morrison Chambers, 32 Nassau Street, Dublin D02 YH68, Ireland, https://eu-contact.penguin.ie.

Random House Children's Books supports the First Amendment and celebrates the right to read.

Photo Credits
AL = Alamy Stock Photo; AS = Adobe Stock; GI = Getty Images; SS = Shutterstock

Cover, matimix/AS; 1, David Pu'u/Corbis RF Stills/GI; 2, Patrick Foto/AS; 3, Sara Lynn Cramb; 4–5, Alistair Berg/Digital Vision/GI; 5, nendrawahyu/AS; 6–7, Dusan Kostic/AS; 6 (LO CTR), Leo Lintang/AS; 6 (LO RT), RTimages/AS; 7 (LO RT), torsak/AS; 7 (LO CTR), Nando Vidal/AS; 7 (LO LE), ParinPIX/AS; 8, Drazen_/E+/GI; 8–9 (BKGRD), ABCDstock/AS; 9, Dimensions/E+/GI; 10, Pollyana Ventura/E+/GI; 10–11 (BKGRD), ABCDstock/AS; 11, Isaiah Love/AS; 12 (RT), WavebreakMediaMicro/AS; 13, Dusan Kostic/AS; 14–15, lunarts_studio/AS; 14–15 (BKGRD), Bernulius/AS; 16 (CTR), dpa picture alliance/AL; 16 (UP), adimas/AS; 16 (LO), Alex Livesey/GI; 17 (UP), Ringo Chiu/SS; 17 (UP) RT, photolink/AS; 17 (CTR INSET), Trinity Mirror/Mirrorpix/AL; 17 (CTR), Pituk/AS; 17 (LO), skynesher/E+/GI; 18, Lordprice Collection/AL; 19, Imago/AL; 20 (UP), chrisdorney/AS; 20 (LO), Reinaldo Coddou H/Pixathl/Sipa/SS; 21, EThamPhoto/AL; 22, Daniel Motz/AL; 23 (UP), Vanessa Carvalho/SS; 23 (LO), Colorsport/SS; 24, JFontan/SS; 25, Focus Pix/SS; 26, Focus on Sport/GI; 27 (UP), Mauricio Duenas Castaneda/EPA-EFE/SS; 27 (LO), Bagu Blanco/Pressinphoto/SS; 28 (UP), Urbanandsport/NurPhoto/SS; 28 (LO), JAMALI Amin/ATP/SPP/SS; 29, Morgan Hancock/SS; 30 (LO), PoppyPix/AS; 30 (UP), Andrey Popov/AS; 31 (LO), PA Images/AL; 31 (UP), matimix/AS; 32 (UP LE), Marcel Schauer/AS; 32 (CTR LE), charnsitr/SS; 32 (LO LE), Mathias Bergeld/BILDBYRÅN/SS; 32 (UP RT), kovop58/AS; 32 (CTR RT), Denys Rudenko/SS; 32 (LO RT), Federico Rostagno/AS

Table of Contents

A Super Sport

On a big green field, two teams play soccer. The players kick a ball back and forth as they dash between two goals.

A player kicks the ball toward the goal. The goalie dives to stop it. But the ball lands in the net: GOAL!

This team is one step closer to winning the match!

Word Score

MATCH: A game or contest played between people or teams

To play a game of soccer, you need two teams. Each team has 11 players on the field. Each team protects their goal area from the other team.

Players score by kicking the ball into the goal using their feet, chest, knees, or head, but not their hands. The ball must cross over the goal line to score a point. The team with the most goals wins!

Suit Up!
To play soccer like a pro, you'll need more than a ball and a big green field. These game-time essentials help keep you safe.

A standard soccer game is 90 minutes long with two 45-minute halves.

Teamwork Makes the Dream Work

Soccer players have different positions, or roles. Each position has its own job during a game. There are four main positions.

Goalkeeper:

Goalkeepers, or goalies, protect the goal. This is the only player allowed to use their hands to stop the ball.

Defender: Defenders work with the goalie to protect the goal and keep the other team from scoring.

Word Score

VERSATILE: Having a lot of uses

Midfielder: This is a versatile role! Midfielders play on both ends of the field to score goals and prevent the opposing team from scoring.

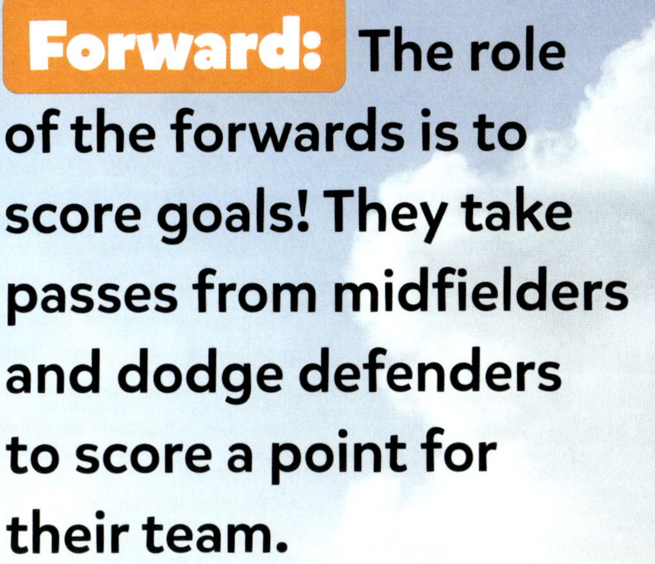

Forward: The role of the forwards is to score goals! They take passes from midfielders and dodge defenders to score a point for their team.

Field FACT

Only 11 players from each team are allowed on the field at one time. But most teams have extra players in case someone gets hurt or needs a break. These players are called substitutes.

Playing It Safe

What happens when a player doesn't follow the rules? Their action is called a foul. The player then receives a penalty, or punishment. Referees give out penalties.

Yellow card: This is a warning given for reckless behavior that could hurt another player or unfairly stops a play from the other team.

Red card: This is the harshest penalty in soccer. It is given for behavior that might seriously hurt or disrespect another player. A player who receives a red card must leave the game. Their team must continue with one less player on the field.

That's a foul! Fouls include disrespectful behavior, kicking, pushing, tripping, or hitting another player.

Word Score

REFEREE: A person who makes sure players follow the rules of a game or sport

Game On!

PENALTY AREA: If a defender commits a foul in their team's penalty area, the opposing team may get the chance to kick the ball into the net. That's called a penalty kick.

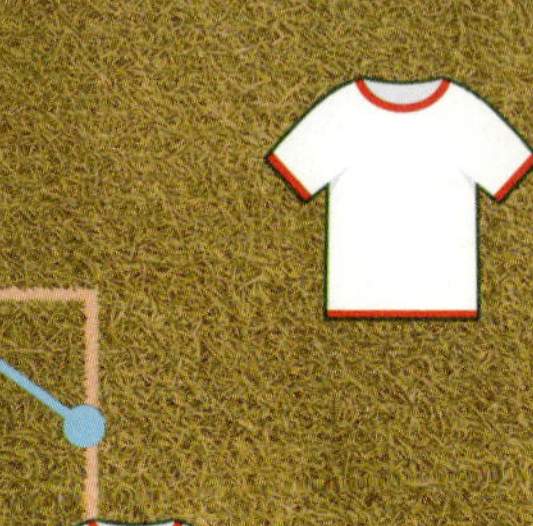

CENTER MARK: This is where players kick the ball to start the game or restart after goals and halftime.

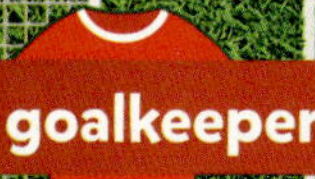

PENALTY MARK: This is where a penalty kick is taken.

HALFWAY LINE: This line divides the field into two sides, one for each team.

SIDELINE: These lines stretch across the length of the field. If a player kicks the ball out of bounds over this line, the opposing team throws the ball onto the field to restart the play.

Here is how a team can organize their 11 players during a soccer game!

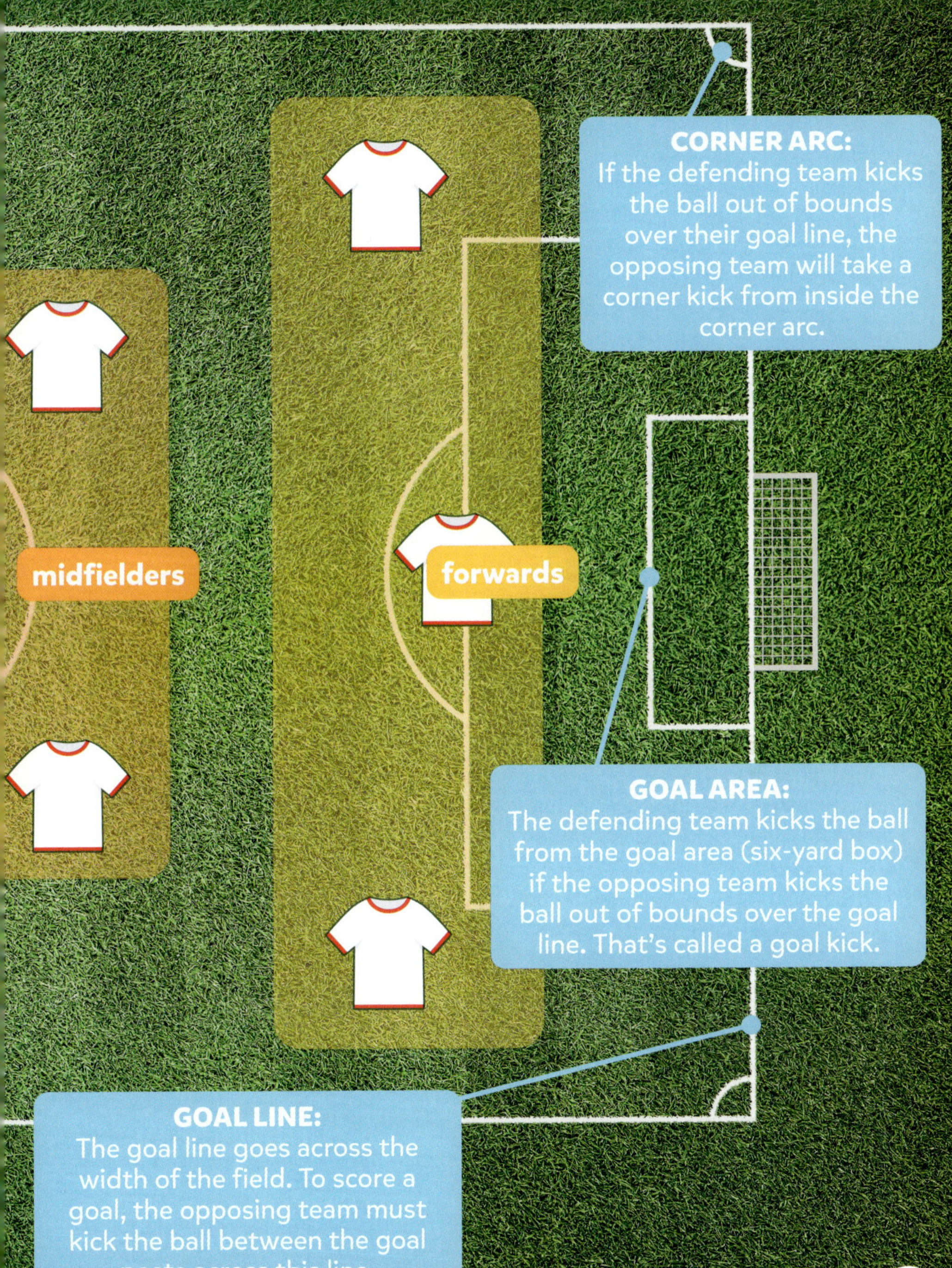

7 Spectacular Soccer Facts

1

In 1954, Hungary set the record for the highest number of combined goals scored in the World Cup with **27 goals total.**

2

Some of the first soccer balls were made of **inflated pig bladders** wrapped in leather.

3

The **top goal scorer** in every World Cup Final receives the **Golden Boot Award.**

4

On average, professional soccer players **run** about **6.2 miles** per game.

5

Some soccer fans bring yellow and red **sticky notes** or signs to games to **call out fouls.**

6

Soccer balls are **black and white** because they were **easier to see** on screen when games first started airing on TV—because most TVs were not in color.

7

Some skilled players score goals using trick shots, like a **bicycle kick.**

Soccer's History

Soccer is one of the oldest sports in history. People have played different versions of soccer all over the world. Some versions are hundreds, even thousands, of years old.

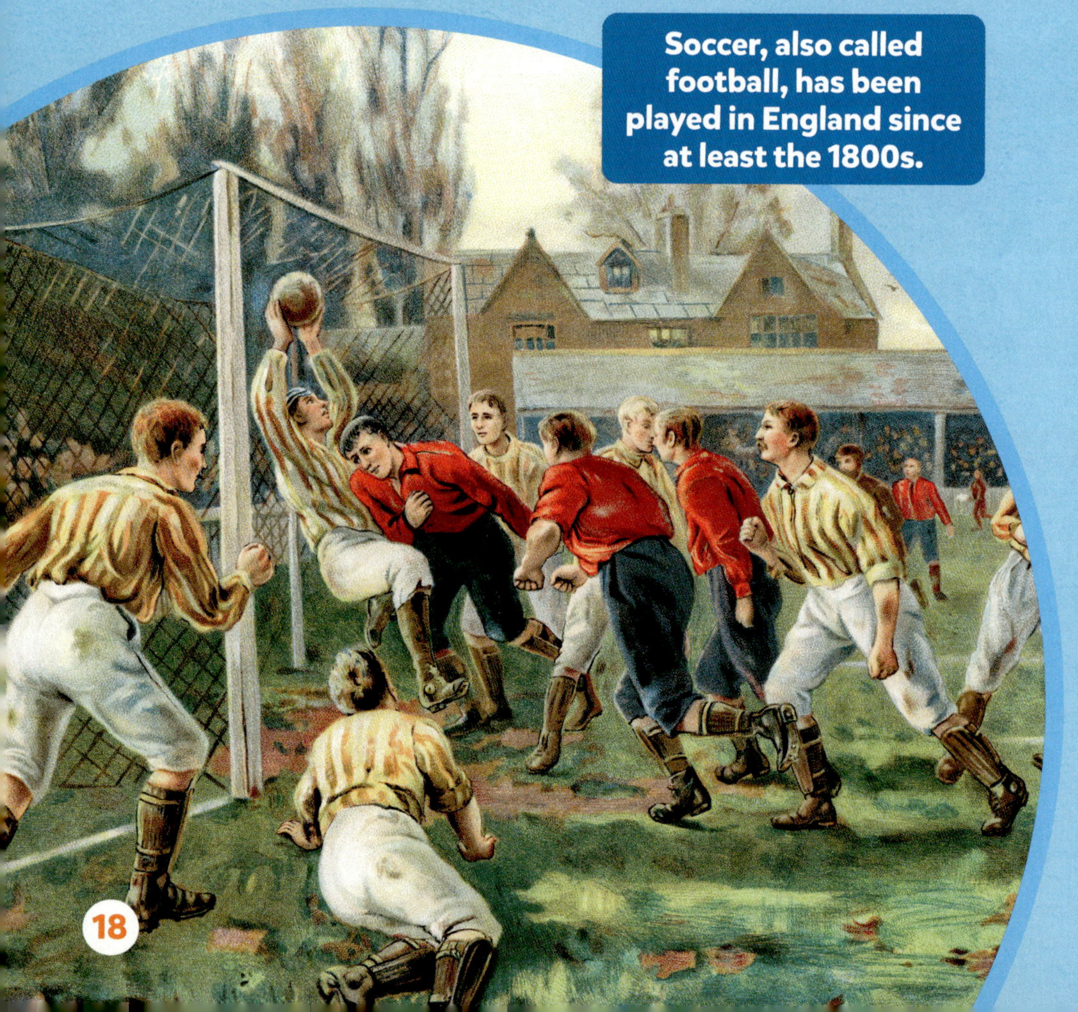

Soccer, also called football, has been played in England since at least the 1800s.

Q What was the athlete's prom called?

A The soccer ball.

Cuju is also called *ts'u-chü*, which means "kick-ball."

One of the early versions of soccer is a Chinese game named *cuju*. Cuju has been played in China for more than 2,000 years!

Organizations to Know

The Football Association was created in England in 1863 to make one set of soccer rules everyone could follow. This is the version of soccer that's most common today.

ENGLAND

Football Association patch

Maracanã Stadium in Rio de Janeiro, Brazil, during the 2014 FIFA World Cup

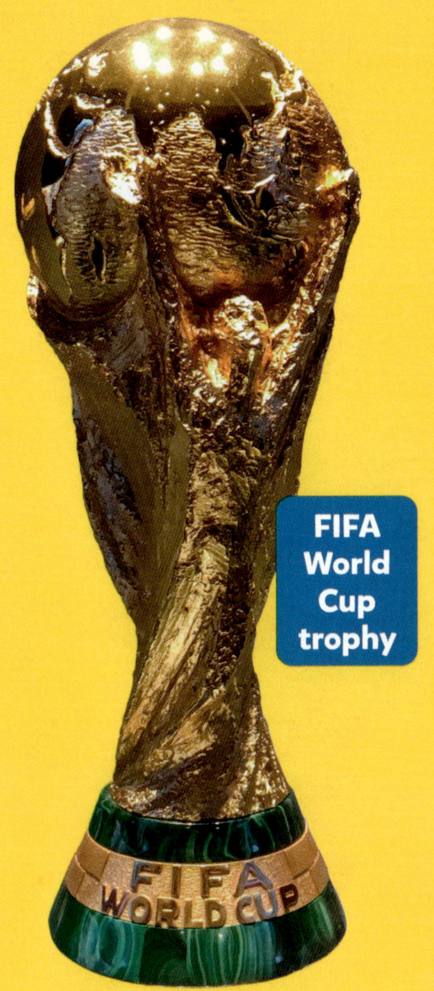

FIFA World Cup trophy

Word Score

INTERNATIONAL: Something that happens between two or more countries

GLOBAL: Involves countries all over the world

Field FACT

Soccer is called football in many parts of the world. The name soccer came from the word "association" in Football Association. First, the sport was called assoccer. Now, in the U.S., it's just called soccer.

There are also global soccer organizations, like the International Federation of Association Football (FIFA). FIFA organizes a global soccer tournament every four years called the World Cup.

Let the Games Begin

Here are some of the most popular professional soccer tournaments:

FIFA World Cup
The first men's FIFA World Cup was hosted in 1930. It is now the most popular professional soccer competition in the world.

The U.S. Women's National Team won the first ever FIFA Women's World Cup in 1991.

Word Score

LEAGUE: A group of teams that play each other

Lionel Messi celebrates with team Argentina after winning the Copa America tournament in 2024.

CONMEBOL Copa America
National teams from South America compete in the Copa America tournament hosted by the South American Football Confederation every four years. Other countries are sometimes invited to participate and even host the games—including the United States!

Cristiano Ronaldo playing for team Real Madrid during the 2018 UEFA Champions League Final.

UEFA Champions League
The Union of European Football Associations (UEFA) organizes the Champions League tournament every year. This is a tournament for the top club teams in Europe. Club teams are different from national teams. National teams represent a country. But players on the same club team can be from all around the world!

Global Popularity

Soccer is the most popular sport in the world! There are millions of players and billions of fans. Soccer is especially popular in the United Kingdom and in European countries like Spain and Italy. Countries in Central and South America are also major soccer hot spots.

Soccer superfans collect trading cards and stickers of their favorite players and join fantasy leagues to create dream teams.

These fans are celebrating team Brazil! Brazil is sometimes called *o país do futebol*, which means "the country of football."

Soccer Superstars

Here are some of the most well-known professional soccer players. These incredible athletes are famous all over the world thanks to their soccer skills!

Pelé
Pelé was a Brazilian soccer player and a national hero for his talents. He was one of the most famous and best-paid athletes in the world. Pelé scored more than 1,000 goals in his lifetime. He began playing at the international level at age 16 and helped Brazil win three World Cup championships.

Pelé is a nickname. His name was actually Edson Arantes do Nascimento.

Linda Caicedo
Caicedo is a Colombian soccer star who began playing professional soccer at 14 years old! She started playing in international tournaments only a few months into her career. She is a top scorer in the Colombian women's soccer league. She also plays for a team in Spain.

Lionel Messi
Messi is an Argentine soccer star. He has won the title of world's best male soccer player eight times! He has played for teams in Spain, Argentina, the United States, and France.

Aitana Bonmatí
Bonmatí is a Spanish soccer player who started playing professionally at age 17. She won the title of world's best female soccer player three times in a row. Bonmatí helped Spain win its first ever Women's World Cup in 2023. She plays for teams in Spain.

Kylian Mbappé
Mbappé is a French soccer player who started in a professional league at age 16. At 19 years old, he became the second teenager ever to score a goal in a World Cup Final. He has played for teams in France and Spain.

Megan Rapinoe

Rapinoe is a former U.S. soccer player from California, U.S.A. During her career, she helped the U.S. win two World Cups. She also won the title of the world's best female soccer player. Rapinoe was the first soccer player to win the U.S. Presidential Medal of Freedom for her work to achieve gender equality in soccer.

Megan Rapinoe is a three-time Olympian! She helped Team USA win a gold and a bronze medal.

Quiz Whiz

1

Which country created the rules for the version of soccer we know today?

A. Brazil
B. Cuba
C. England
D. Spain

2

What does FIFA stand for?

A. International Forum of Association Football
B. International Federation of Association Football
C. International Federation of Assoccer
D. International Faculty of Association Football

3

How many players from one soccer team play on the field during a game?

A. 7
B. 17
C. 23
D. 11

4

Which player is allowed to touch the ball with their hands?

A. midfielder
B. goalie
C. forward
D. defender

What is the harshest penalty in soccer?

A. red card
B. blue card
C. time-out
D. yellow card

original World Cup trophy design

When was the first World Cup tournament?

A. 1990
B. 1912
C. 1900
D. 1930

Which of these players scored more than 1,000 goals in their lifetime?

A. Kylian Mbappé
B. Pelé
C. Megan Rapinoe
D. Lionel Messi

7

Answers: 1. C, 2. B, 3. D, 4. B, 5. A, 6. D, 7. B

Glossary

Global
Involves countries all over the world

International
Something that happens between two or more countries

League
A group of teams that play each other

Match
A game or contest played between people or teams

Referee
A person who makes sure players follow the rules of a game or sport

Versatile
Having a lot of uses

National Geographic Kids Readers

for curious kids at every reading level!

Pre-reader • Ready to read

Level 1 Co-reader • Starting to read together

Level 1 • Starting to read

Reading independently

Level 2 books are perfect for kids who are ready for longer sentences and more complex vocabulary. New words are defined on the page, but occasional adult help might be welcome.

Level 3 • Fluent reader

Manufactured in the United States of America

rhcbooks.com | @randomhousekids

US $5.99 / $7.99 CAN

ISBN 978-1-4263-7802-7